Level
2

THE NATURE KIDS GUIDE TO

KOALAS

DAVID ANDERSON

LP Media Inc. Publishing
Text copyright © 2026 by LP Media Inc.
All rights reserved.

No part of this book may be reproduced or transmitted in any form or by any means, electronic or mechanical, including photocopying, recording, or by an information storage and retrieval system — except by a reviewer who may quote brief passages in a review to be printed in a magazine or newspaper — without permission in writing from the publisher.

For information address LP Media Inc. Publishing,
30012 Variolite St NW, Princeton MN 55371
www.lpmedia.org

Publication Data

Koalas
The Nature Kid's Guide to Koalas — First edition.

Summary: "Learn all about Koalas, the Nature Kid Way"
— Provided by publisher.

ISBN: 979-8-89818-114-7

[1. Koalas – Non-Fiction] I. Title.

Title: The Nature Kid's Guide to Koalas

CONTENTS

TREE TOPS

DID YOU KNOW?

Koalas are not bears. They are marsupials. This means mothers carry babies in a pouch. Kangaroos and wombats are also marsupials.

Crunch! A koala chews a leaf high in a tree. It holds on with sharp claws.

Koalas live high up in tall trees. These trees have long, thin leaves that smell fresh and strong. The forests feel quiet and peaceful.

The air can be warm or cool. Some days are dry. Other days bring soft rain. Koalas need many trees close together. Each koala picks its own set of trees to call home.

Koalas rest in the spots where branches meet. Their thick, soft fur keeps them cozy on chilly nights. The trees give them food, shelter, and safety. Tree tops are the perfect home for these fuzzy animals.

AUSSIE ANIMALS

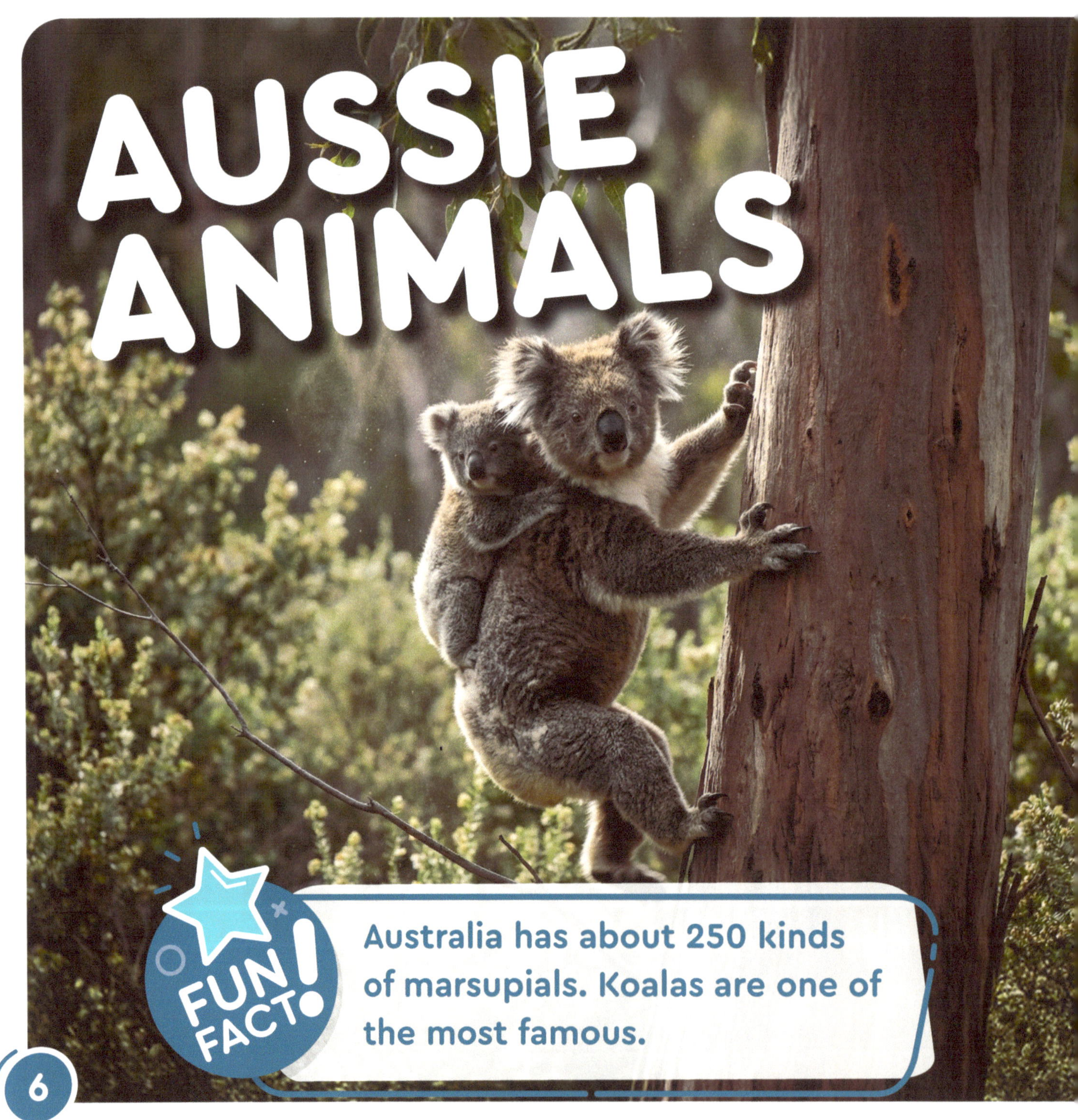

Australia has about 250 kinds of marsupials. Koalas are one of the most famous.

Rustle! A koala climbs between branches. The leaves shake as it moves.

Koalas only live in Australia. They live on the east coast. You can find them from Queensland in the north to Victoria in the south.

Northern koalas live in Queensland. They are smaller and have less fur. The warm weather means they do not need thick coats. Southern koalas live in Victoria and South Australia. They are bigger and fluffier. Their thick fur keeps them warm in the cooler winters.

No wild koalas live in any other country. They need special eucalyptus trees to eat. Only Australia has the right trees growing in the wild.

Southern koalas can weigh twice as much as northern koalas. The cold weather makes them grow bigger and fluffier.

Thump! A koala drops onto a low branch. Its round body settles in leaves.

Koalas grow to be about two to three feet long. Adults weigh about 9 to 33 pounds. That is about the size of a small dog.

Male koalas are larger than females. A big male can be twice the size of a small female.

Their size is perfect for life in the trees. Koalas are small enough to climb out on thin branches to reach the best leaves. But they are big enough to hold on tight in strong winds. Their lean, muscular bodies help them grip tree trunks and move from branch to branch with ease.

FUZZY
FEATURES

Snap! A koala scratches its back on rough bark. It feels good.

Koalas have thick, woolly fur. The fur is gray or brown on their backs. Their bellies are white or cream colored. This thick coat keeps them dry in the rain.

Koalas have large, spoon-shaped noses. The nose is black and leathery. It stands out on their fluffy face. Big, fuzzy ears stand out on top of their head.

Koalas have two thumbs on each front paw. This helps them grip branches tightly.

Koala fingerprints look almost exactly like human fingerprints!

SUPER SNIFFERS

Sniff! A koala smells the air. Its big nose wiggles.

Koalas have an amazing sense of smell. Their large noses help them find the right leaves to eat. They can smell which leaves are safe.

Koalas also use smell to find other koalas. Males leave scent marks on trees.

The smell tells other koalas who lives nearby. Baby koalas learn these smells from their mothers.

Koalas use their noses to choose from over 600 types of eucalyptus leafs.

STAY SAFE

Screech! A koala calls out a warning. It wraps its arms around a branch.

Koalas stay safe by living high in trees. Most predators cannot reach them up there. Their gray fur also helps by blending in with tree bark.

Koalas have sharp claws on all four paws. These claws can scratch attackers. The claws also help koalas climb away fast.

If a koala senses danger, it hugs the tree trunk tightly and stays very still. From the ground, it looks like a bump on the tree. This makes it hard for predators to spot them.

A koala's bottom has extra thick fur. This padding protects it on hard branches.

15

LEAF
LOVERS

Chomp! A koala bites into a leaf and chews it slowly.

Koalas only eat **eucalyptus** leaves. These leaves are tough. They are hard to digest. Most animals cannot eat them. Koalas have a special gut. It breaks down the leaves.

Eucalyptus leaves do not have much energy. This is why koalas move so slowly. They rest a lot to save energy.

Koalas eat about one pound of leaves each day. These leaves also give koalas most of the water they need.

Koalas smell like cough drops from all the leaves they eat!

BELLOWING KOALAS

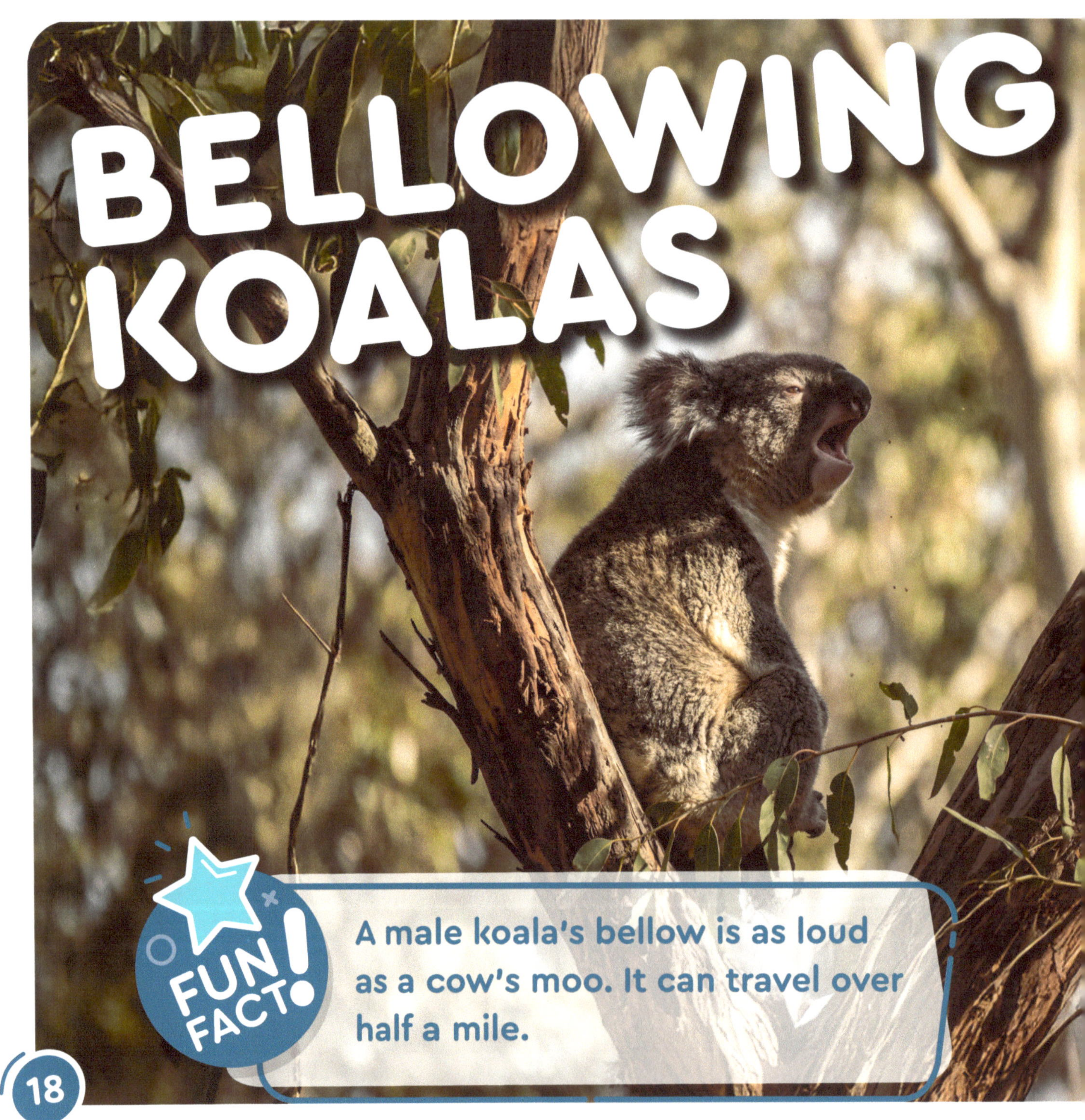

A male koala's bellow is as loud as a cow's moo. It can travel over half a mile.

Bellow! A male koala makes a loud, deep sound.

Koalas talk to each other with sounds. Males make a deep bellowing call. This sound is very loud. It can be heard far away through the forest.

The bellow sounds like a burp mixed with a snore. Males make this sound to show where they live. Other males hear it and stay away.

Females make sounds too. They can scream, wail, or grunt. Baby koalas make squeaking sounds. Mother koalas click softly to their babies. Each sound means something different.

WATCH OUT

Growl! A dingo looks up at a tree. A koala sits still.

Koalas have several **predators**. Dingoes and large owls hunt them. Pythons can catch koalas too.

Dogs are a big danger to koalas. When koalas walk on the ground, dogs may attack them. Koalas can run fast if scared.

Eagles can grab young koalas from trees. Wedge-tailed eagles use their strong talons to snatch them. Baby koalas are most at risk from these birds.

Cars hit many koalas each year when they cross roads at night to find food.

CLIMB HIGH

Whoosh! A koala scrambles up a trunk, climbing fast to safety.

Koalas climb trees to stay safe. When danger comes, they go higher. Their sharp claws grip the bark tightly.

This fast climbing helps them escape danger. They use their strong arms to pull themselves up. Their rough paw pads also help them hold on.

High branches are the safest spots. Most predators cannot climb trees to catch koalas.

Koalas can climb down trees headfirst by turning their back feet around to grip the bark.

SLOW MOVERS

Click! A koala grips a branch. It moves one paw slowly.

Koalas usually move slowly to save energy. Their leafy diet gives them little energy to spare.

On the ground, koalas walk on all fours. They move their short legs one at a time. But they can run fast if needed.

Koalas spend most of their time sitting still. They only move to find food or a new tree.

Koalas can run as fast as a human when they need to escape danger on the ground.

SLEEP STARS

Snarl! A koala yawns wide and its eyes slowly close.

Koalas sleep up to 22 hours each day. They rest in tree forks. They curl into tight balls on branches.

Sleeping saves energy. Eucalyptus leaves are hard to digest. Resting helps their bodies break down the tough food.

Koalas are most active at night. They wake up to eat. They move around at dawn and dusk too.

Koalas sleep so deeply that they sometimes fall out of trees and keep sleeping on the ground!

LONER LIFE
28

A koala sits alone in a tall eucalyptus tree. It watches below.

Koalas live alone most of the time. Each koala has its own trees. This is called it's **home range**.

Male koalas mark trees with a scent. This warns other males to stay away. It also draws females near. Females have their own home areas too.

Koalas only meet to mate. Then they go back to living alone.

Koalas poop over 100 tiny pellets every day. They even poop while they sleep!

BELLOWING BOYS

Rumble! A male koala makes a deep bellow. It echoes through the trees.

Male koalas bellow a lot during mating season. The bellows rumble like thunder. You can hear them far away.

Mating season is from September to February in Australia. The bellowing helps the females find them.

Females listen to the calls. They can tell males apart just by their bellow.

Male koalas have a special voice organ in their throat that makes their bellowing sound.

TINY JOEYS

Squeak! A tiny pink joey hangs tightly onto it's mother.

A newborn koala is called a **joey**. It is only the size of a jellybean and is born blind with no fur.

The tiny joey crawls into its mother's pouch right after birth. It stays inside for about six months, where the pouch keeps it warm and safe.

Inside the pouch, the joey drinks milk and grows. It develops eyes, ears, and soft gray fur. Then it will be ready to see the world.

A joey weighs less than one gram at birth. That is lighter than a paperclip.

POUCH POWER

Grunt! A Joey holds onto it's mother's neck while she climbs up.

Koala mothers carry their babies for a long time. After leaving the pouch, joeys ride on their mother's back and hold on tight to her fur.

Mothers also feed their joeys a special food called pap. This soft paste comes from the mother's body. It helps joeys learn to digest tough eucalyptus leaves.

Joeys stay with their mothers for about one year. Then they find their own trees to live in.

A koala's pouch opens downward, not upward like a kangaroo's.

BURNING
BUSH

Crack! Smoke fills the air. A koala clings to a charred tree.

Wildfires are a big threat to koalas. Australia has many bushfires each year. These fires burn eucalyptus forests. Koalas live in these trees.

Koalas move slowly. They cannot run from fast flames. Many koalas die in big fires.

Fires also burn the trees koalas need. Without leaves to eat, they can starve. It can take years for forests to grow back. Until then, koalas must search far and wide for new homes.

In 2019–2020, Australian bushfires killed tens of thousands of koalas. Some areas lost half their koalas.

HELPING HANDS

Splash! A rescued koala drinks cool water from a bowl.

Many people help koalas. Rescuers save sick koalas. They save hurt koalas too. They take them to animal hospitals.

Vets care for the koalas. The koalas get well. Then they go back to the wild.

Groups plant new eucalyptus trees. This gives koalas more homes. It gives them more food. Every tree helps.

Some hospitals use special koala mittens to protect burned paws while they heal.

GLOSSARY

marsupial
An animal whose mother carries her baby in a pouch on her belly.

predator
An animal that hunts and eats other animals.

joey
A baby koala or other baby marsupial.

eucalyptus
A type of tall tree that grows in Australia and has leaves that koalas eat.

home range
The group of trees where one koala lives and finds its food.

www.ingramcontent.com/pod-product-compliance
Lightning Source LLC
Chambersburg PA
CBHW041615110726
48005CB00002B/406